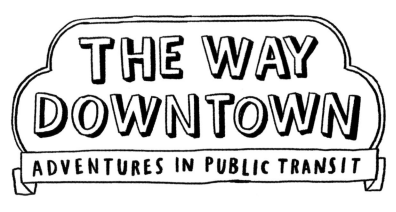

For my sons, Brody and Boris, and for my nephews and nieces, Chaim, Rochel, Chaya, Tova, Boozik, Ethel, Hershey and Shmulie. And for my parents, who have taught me everything. —I.G.

To my two favorite humans: Katrin and Allister — M.L.

Text © 2017 Inna Gertsberg
Illustrations © 2017 Mike Lowery

Kids Can Press gratefully acknowledges the financial support of the Government of Ontario, through the Ontario Media Development Corporation; the Ontario Arts Council; the Canada Council for the Arts; and the Government of Canada, through the CBF, for our publishing activity.

Published in Canada and the U.S. by Kids Can Press Ltd.
25 Dockside Drive, Toronto, ON M5A 0B5

Kids Can Press is a Corus Entertainment Inc. company

www.kidscanpress.com

The artwork in this book was rendered with pencil, pen and ink and digital techniques.
The text is set in Shaky Hand Some comic.

Edited by Yasemin Uçar
Designed by Marie Bartholomew

Printed and bound in Shenzhen, China, in 3/2017 by Imago

CM 17 0 9 8 7 6 5 4 3 2 1

Library and Archives Canada Cataloguing in Publication

Gertsberg, Inna, author
    The way downtown : adventures in public transit
/ Inna Gertsberg ; illustrator: Mike Lowery.

ISBN 978-1-77138-552-7 (hardcover)

1. Local transit – Juvenile literature. I. Lowery, Mike, 1980–, illustrator II. Title.

HE4211.G47 2017   j388.4   C2016-907459-5

THE WAY DOWNTOWN

ADVENTURES IN PUBLIC TRANSIT

INNA GERTSBERG
MIKE LOWERY

Kids Can Press

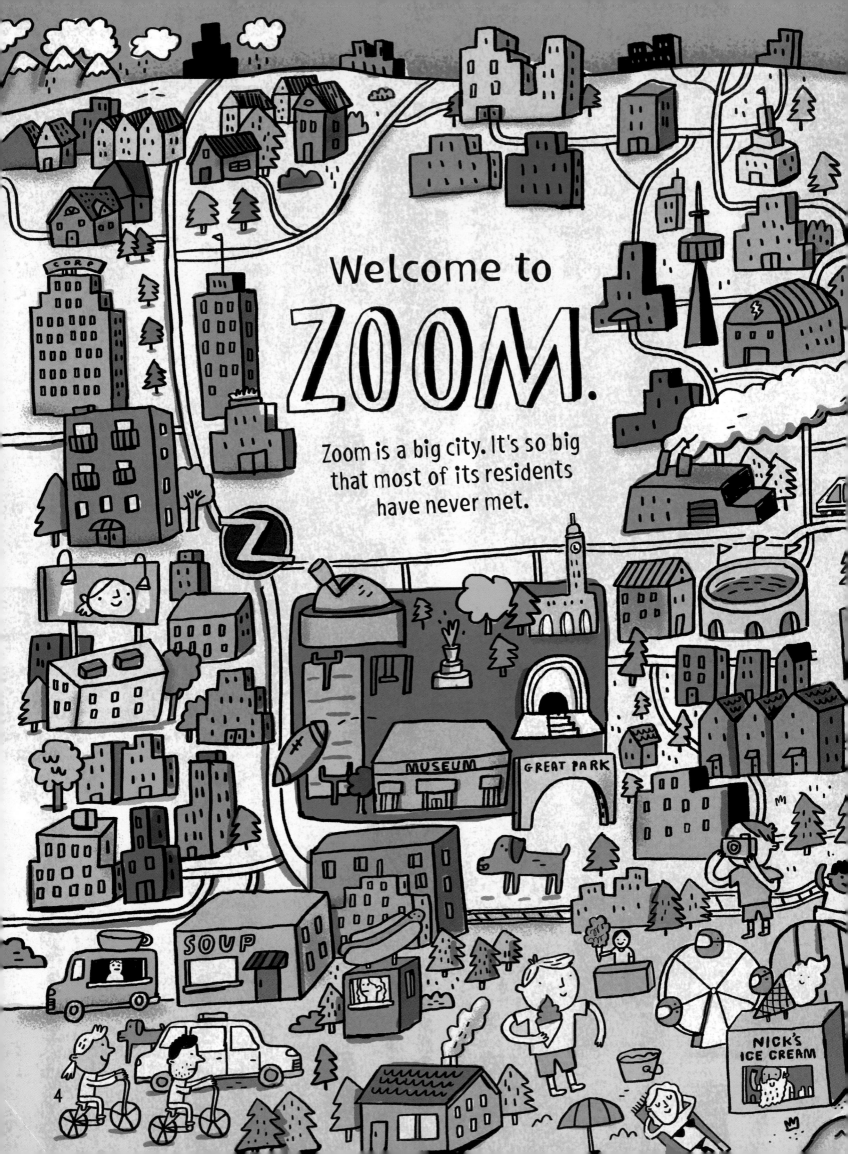

Welcome to
ZOOM.

Zoom is a big city. It's so big that most of its residents have never met.

MUSEUM

GREAT PARK

SOUP

NICK'S ICE CREAM

POPULATION (HUMANS): 3 000 001
POPULATION (ANIMALS): NOT EXACTLY KNOWN

PARKS: 1413
MUSEUMS: 22
SCHOOLS: 458
HOSPITALS: 24

OBSERVATORIES: 1
ICE CREAM SHOPS: 29
COOKIE FACTORIES: 1
SWIMMING POOLS: 114
LIBRARIES: 98
ROLLER COASTERS: 1
SUBWAY STATIONS: 68

TRAIN STATIONS: 16
BUS STOPS: 9013
LIGHT RAIL TRANSIT
STOPS: 700
AIRPORTS: 1
FERRIES: 2

THE ZANIES

MASTERS OF OUTSIDE ARTS
The Zanies are masters of the didgeridoo, juggling and squeezing into very small spaces. They perform for crowds in the streets of Zoom. The Zanies live in a house uptown.

AGENT RYBKA

SECRET AGENT 008
Agent Theodore Rybka is a spy. He has just arrived at Zoom International Airport on a top secret mission. Agent Rybka really likes tea, and he does not like crowds.

ROBBIE

1ST GRADER & PHOTOGRAPHER
Robbie is visiting from a small beach town very far away. He's staying with his aunt Raisa, who lives in an apartment on Zoom's west side. Robbie likes taking pictures of animals.

Every day, about two million Zoomies take buses, subways, trains, light rail and ferries to get where they're going. All of these things that move people around the city are called **PUBLIC TRANSIT.**

Public transit has its own map, its own rules, even its own language. It also has its own stories. The closer you ZOOM, the more you see ...

BORIS

GUY'S BEST FRIEND
Boris and his best friend, Guy, live in an apartment on the east side of the city. Boris is a guide dog. He helps Guy get around Zoom safely. He knows a lot of road and transit rules.

DR. BRODY

DIRECTOR OF EXPEDITIONS, EARTH MUSEUM
Dr. Brody lives in a house on the Island. As a scientist and explorer, she often travels to distant corners of the world. At home, she likes to sleep in a tent in her backyard and ride one of her five bikes.

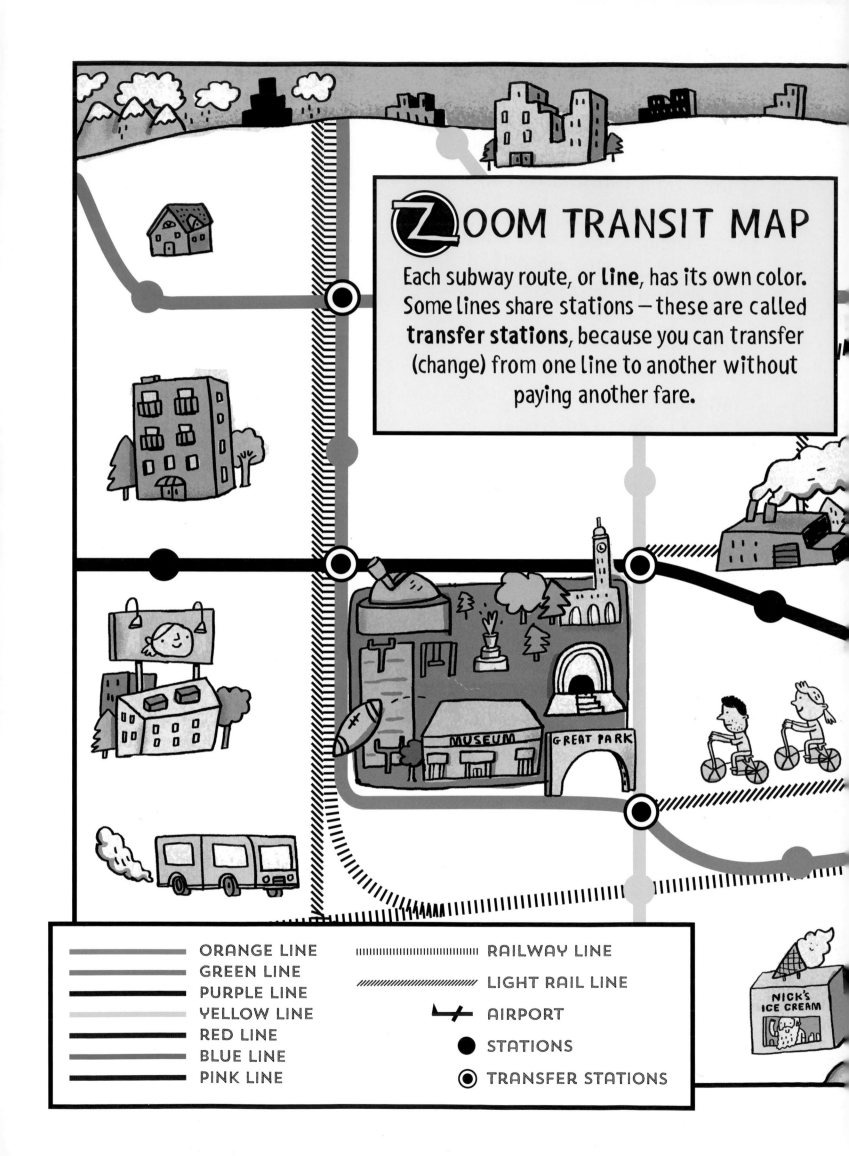

ZOOM TRANSIT MAP

Each subway route, or **line**, has its own color. Some lines share stations — these are called **transfer stations**, because you can transfer (change) from one line to another without paying another fare.

MUSEUM

GREAT PARK

NICK'S ICE CREAM

——— ORANGE LINE	⫶⫶⫶⫶⫶⫶ RAILWAY LINE
——— GREEN LINE	⁄⁄⁄⁄⁄⁄⁄ LIGHT RAIL LINE
——— PURPLE LINE	✈ AIRPORT
——— YELLOW LINE	
——— RED LINE	● STATIONS
——— BLUE LINE	◉ TRANSFER STATIONS
——— PINK LINE	

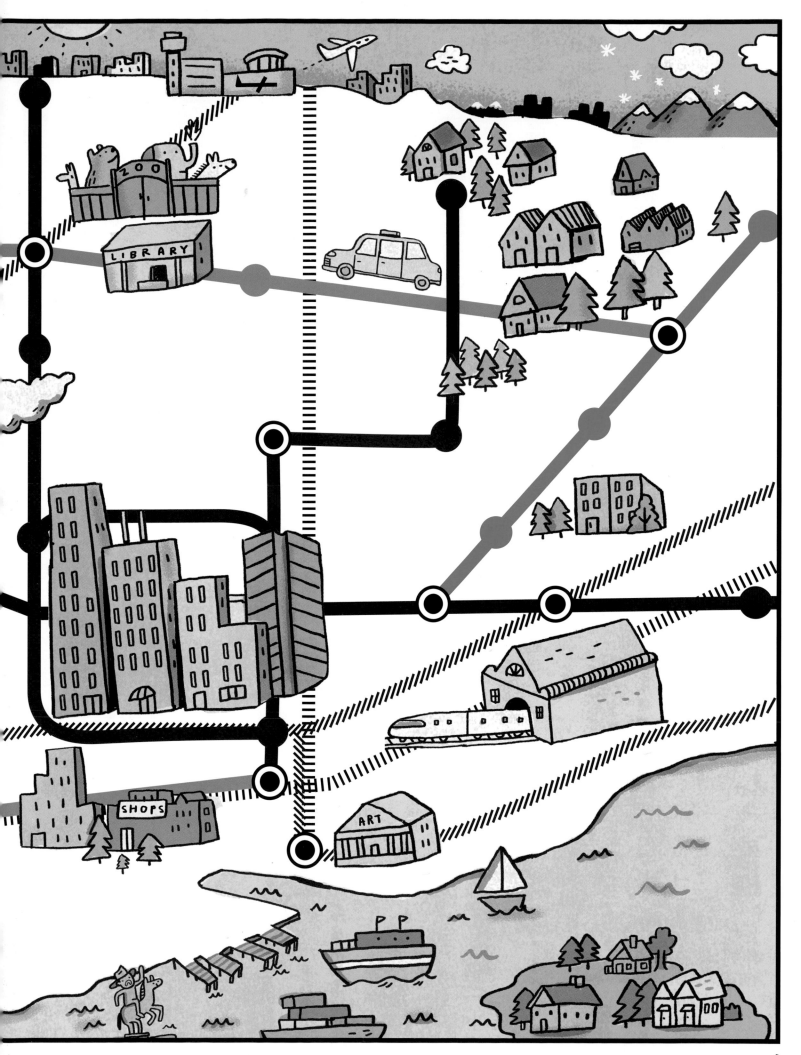

DR. BRODY doesn't like getting up early. But this morning, she can't wait to go to work. In her backpack, she has something very special she discovered on her trip to China.

To get downtown, Dr. Brody rides her bike, takes a ferry, then rides her bike again.

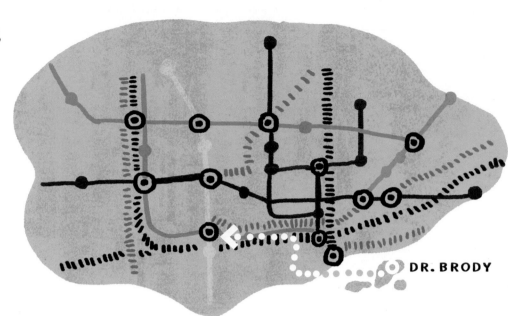

It's still chilly from the night. The wind is keeping most passengers on the bottom deck. But Dr. Brody heads straight for the top.

FERRY CAPTAIN

← ALL FERRIES ARE EQUIPPED WITH **LIFE RINGS**, LIFE **VESTS** AND OTHER SAFETY GEAR.

YOU GUYS MUST BE HUNGRY.

DR. BRODY ALWAYS BUYS HER **FERRY TICKET** FROM THE TICKET **VENDING MACHINE.** HER BIKE TRAVELS FOR **FREE!**

TICKETS

THE **FERRY** IS A SMALL **SHIP** THAT MOVES **PASSENGERS** FROM THE **ISLAND** TO THE **CITY** AND BACK, 365 **DAYS** A YEAR.

11

WATERFRONT PARK

AND AWAY SHE GOES!

FERRY DOCKS

THIS **FERRY** IS **DOUBLE-ENDED**, WHICH MEANS IT CAN GO BACK AND FORTH **WITHOUT** HAVING TO **TURN AROUND**.

SOME **ZOOMIES** HAVE THEIR OWN **BOATS**. YOU NEED A SPECIAL **LICENSE** TO DRIVE ONE.

CLICK!

DOES ANYONE REMEMBER WHICH CONTAINER THE CHEESE IS IN?

ZOOM'S FIRST **MAYOR**, YAKOV STROGANOFF, WAS A BRILLIANT CITY PLANNER WHO LOVED **HORSES** AND SILLY HATS.

WATER TAXI

CARGO SHIP

The ferry takes 22 minutes to reach Zoom Harbor. Dr. Brody is never bored, because there is lots to see on the way. But today, it's what she has in her backpack that keeps her busy. They sure are hungry!

THERE ARE 2490 PASSENGERS ON BOARD THIS VISITING CRUISE SHIP!

Dr. Brody has been riding the streets of Zoom since before there were bike lanes. It's a lot like trekking through the jungle — you really have to pay attention.

Under the bridge ... Across the tracks ... Past the bus terminal ...

BIKE LANES CAN ONLY BE USED BY BICYCLES. NO CARS ALLOWED!

ZOOMER STATION

ZOOMER IS THE CITY'S BIKE SHARING SYSTEM. BIKES CAN BE RENTED AND RETURNED TO ANY ZOOMER STATION IN THE SYSTEM, 24 HOURS A DAY, 365 DAYS A YEAR.

... And then through ... the marble gate of Zoom's Great Park.

The Museum is still closed and Ben the security guard isn't answering his phone. She'll have to wait.

Inside Dr. Brody's backpack, there's only gentle snoring.

Today, ROBBIE is going on a subway for the first time! Aunt Raisa says it's like a whole city underground, with long dark tunnels. She also says there are animals down there. Even pigeons!

To get downtown, Robbie and Aunt Raisa take a bus, then transfer to the orange line and ride the subway the rest of the way.

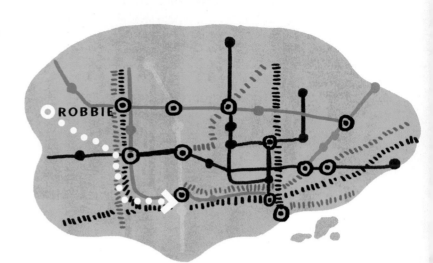

The bus runs every seven minutes on weekdays and every half hour on weekends. Today is Tuesday so the wait is short and the bus is full of Zoomies going to work.

AS A KID **UNDER 10** YEARS OLD, ROBBIE CAN **RIDE ZOOM** TRANSIT FOR **FREE**, BUT AUNT RAISA HAS TO PAY.

HOW MANY STOPS UNTIL THE SUBWAY?

CAN I PUSH THE STOP BUTTON?

IS THIS OUR STOP?

ALL OF ZOOM'S BUSES HAVE **RAMPS** TO BE **ACCESSIBLE** FOR EVERYONE.

THIS STATION IS WHAT'S CALLED A
TRANSIT HUB – IT'S WHERE
VARIOUS MODES OF TRANSPORTATION
(BUS, LIGHT RAIL, SUBWAY) MEET.

JAKE!

The subway station smells like shoes and cinnamon. A loud voice announces that the train will be delayed—signal problem. Some people grumble. But then a service crew shows up. They jump right onto the tracks and disappear in the tunnel. Robbie wishes they'd take him along so he could look for subway mice.

The subway platform is really crowded! Will everyone fit?

FINALLY!

← THIS **LIGHT RAIL** TRAIN HAS **NO DRIVER!** IT'S OPERATED BY A **COMPUTER.**

I'M HUNGRY!

TRANSIT **REPAIR** CREWS MAKE SURE EVERYTHING INSIDE THE SYSTEM **WORKS PROPERLY** – TRANSIT SIGNALS, **ESCALATORS, TRACKS, TRAINS** AND MUCH MORE.

TO SUBWAY

AGENT THEODORE RYBKA (also known as Agent 008) has an important package to deliver to Agent 006 in downtown Zoom. This is his first visit to the city, but Agent Rybka is already in disguise. One can never be too careful!

The quickest and most direct way to the city from the airport is by a special airport express train — but Agent Rybka has a better idea ...

To get downtown, Agent Rybka takes a very confusing and indirect route, in case he's being followed. It includes two train rides, lots of walking and three subway rides.

AGENT RYBKA

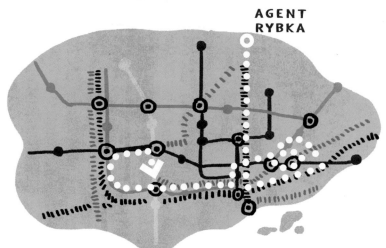

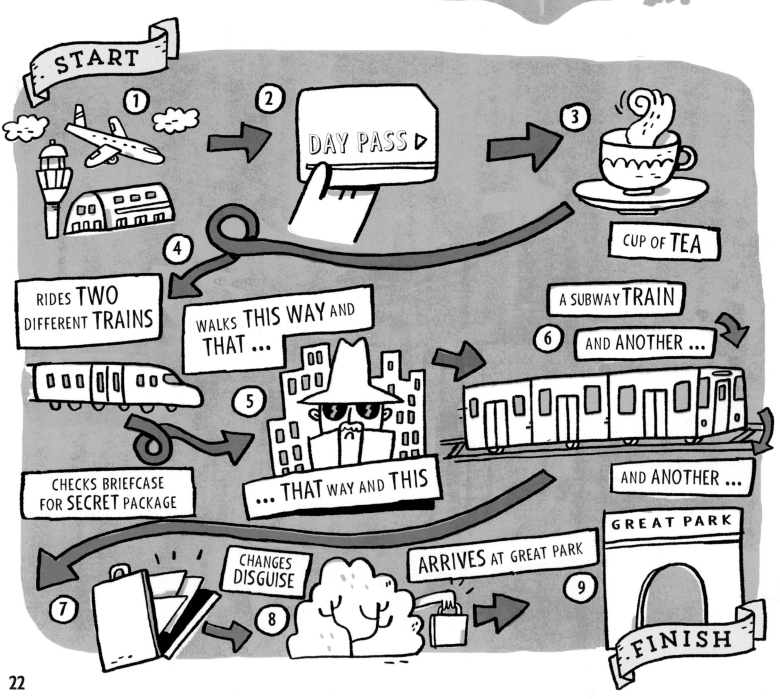

START

1

2 DAY PASS ▷

3 CUP OF TEA

4 RIDES **TWO** DIFFERENT **TRAINS**

WALKS **THIS WAY** AND **THAT** ...

5

A SUBWAY **TRAIN**

6 AND ANOTHER ...

CHECKS BRIEFCASE FOR **SECRET** PACKAGE

... **THAT** WAY AND **THIS**

AND ANOTHER ...

GREAT PARK

7

CHANGES DISGUISE

8

ARRIVES AT GREAT PARK

9

FINISH

The east side of Zoom is one of the oldest parts of the city. It's easy to get lost here without using a map or asking for directions. Agent Rybka doesn't like to involve strangers in his missions, but he'll have to make an exception.

Changing trains and getting lost mean that Agent Rybka's arrival downtown will be delayed.

After a long and befuddling ride, Agent Rybka arrives downtown. The most important stage of the mission is about to take place. But first he'll need to adjust his disguise to make sure he blends in.

A spy's life isn't easy. You have to keep lots of secrets. Even the name of your cat ... because if they find your cat, they will find you.

It's only Tuesday but THE ZANIES have already had a big week. School's over, which means show season has begun! This summer, they're moving their act to Great Park in the hope of attracting a bigger audience.

To get downtown, the Zanies take a subway along the orange line.

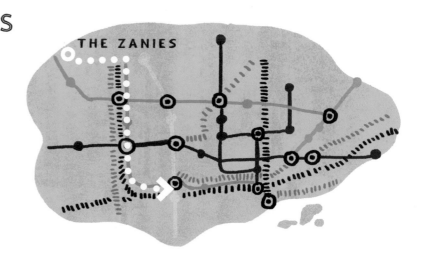

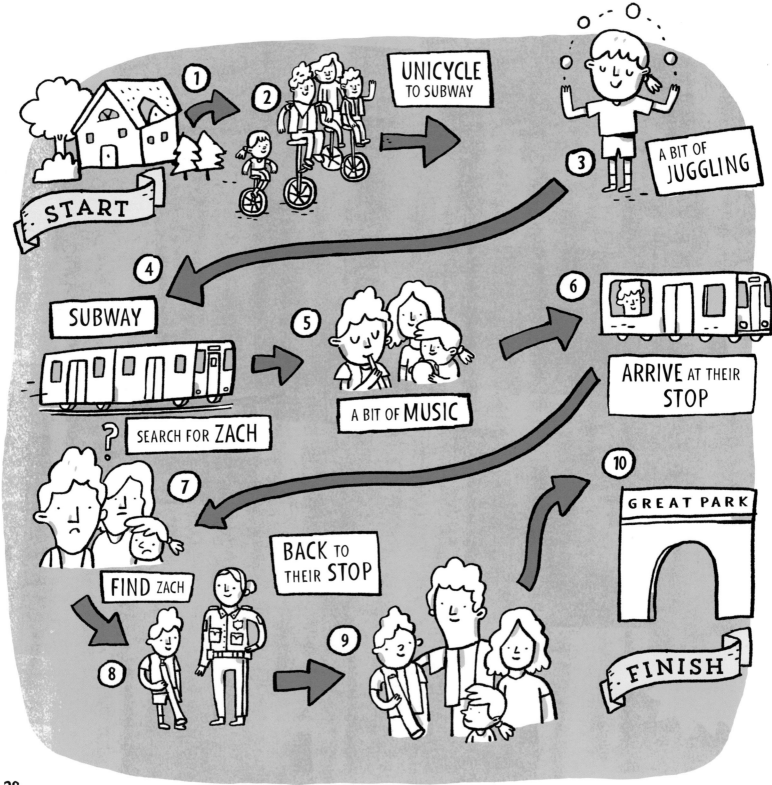

The Zanies have monthly transit passes that let them ride anywhere they need to go, every day, for a month. Since they have performed all over Zoom, they really know their way around the city. Even taxi drivers sometimes ask the Zanies for directions!

TICKET TYPES

 A SINGLE-RIDE TICKET BUYS A RIDE FROM ONE PART OF ZOOM TO ANOTHER.

 A TRANSFER LETS YOU CHANGE FROM ONE FORM OF TRANSIT TO ANOTHER ON A SINGLE FARE.

 A DAY PASS BUYS UNLIMITED RIDES IN ALL DIRECTIONS AND ON ALL FORMS OF TRANSIT FOR ONE DAY.

A MONTHLY PASS IS LIKE A DAY PASS, BUT FOR A WHOLE MONTH!

 A SMART CARD IS A PRE-PAID CARD, WHICH STORES MONEY SO THAT THE CARD CAN BE USED INSTEAD OF CASH OR TICKETS. PASSENGERS TAP THEIR CARD ON A SPECIAL READER TO DEDUCT THEIR FARE. SMART, RIGHT?

ZOOMIES OVER 65 AND STUDENTS OVER 10 PAY A REDUCED FARE.

ZOOMIES UNDER 10 RIDE FOR FREE.

The Zanies like performing in subway stations. The sound is big, and the audience is different every time.

DING! DING!

♪

TRAIN'S COMING!

PRIORITY SEATS ARE FOR PASSENGERS WITH SPECIAL NEEDS, TO GIVE THEM EASY ACCESS TO THE DOOR.

The Zanies arrive at their stop, but someone has forgotten to get off the train!

Transit SECURITY OFFICERS KEEP PASSENGERS SAFE, AND SOMETIMES HELP THEM FIND THEIR LOST SIBLINGS.

IF YOU LEAVE SOMETHING BEHIND ON A BUS OR TRAIN, IT USUALLY ENDS UP IN THE LOST AND FOUND (UNLESS IT'S A LOST PERSON!).

First Zach forgets to remember his stop. Then he forgets to remember that he's lost!

It's rehearsal time! Each trick requires skill, coordination and props. And for all four Zanies to be present!

BORIS wakes up to the noise of the recycling truck. He knows it's a recycling truck because he can hear glass bottles rattling and clinking. The radio comes on, too. And then the phone rings! Today, they're meeting Leslie at the park.

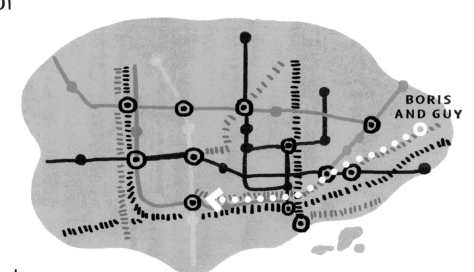

BORIS AND GUY

To get downtown, Boris and Guy walk two blocks to the light rail stop and take a westbound light rail train.

START

1

2 WALK TO LIGHT RAIL STOP

3 GUIDE GUY AROUND OBSTACLES

4 FIND PRIORITY SEAT FOR GUY

5 RIDE THE LIGHT RAIL

6 A LITTLE SCRATCH BEHIND THE EAR

7 STILL ON THE TRAIN

8 FIND EXIT

9 IGNORE DISTRACTIONS

10 FINISH

GREAT PARK

SNIFF SNIFF

Boris's job is to make sure that Guy is always safe.

ALL ZOOM TRANSIT INFORMATION BOARDS INCLUDE **BRAILLE** FOR PEOPLE WHO ARE **VISUALLY IMPAIRED.**

ALL TRAIN AND SUBWAY **PLATFORMS** HAVE A **YELLOW STRIP** WITH A RAISED TEXTURE SO THAT PEOPLE CAN FEEL WHERE **THE EDGE** OF THE PLATFORM IS AND **STAY SAFE.**

It's Tuesday morning at Great Park ...

Dr. Brody is about to deliver her exciting discovery to the Museum (if she catches them!).

Robbie is about to snap a photo of an extremely unusual creature.

Theodore Rybka is about to complete his top secret mission.

The world's greatest outdoor performance is about to take place.

40

GLOSSARY

Band shell
A stage in the shape of a large shell. The shell shape makes music sound better when it's played outside.

Bike share
A public transit service that lets you pick up a bike at a special station in one part of the city and drop it off in another, for a small fare. The largest bike sharing system is in Hangzhou, China, with almost 2700 stations and close to 80 000 bikes!

Braille
Braille is a special written language for people who are blind. Each letter and number is a different pattern of six raised dots, which can be felt by the fingertips. The language was invented by a Frenchman named Louis Braille.

Cargo ship
A ship that carries goods (cargo) from one port (harbor city or town) to another. Cargo includes everything from refrigerators to pineapples to books — like the one you are holding in your hands!

Cruise ship
A ship that takes people on long pleasure trips to destinations around the world. Cruise ships are floating hotels that have restaurants, entertainment and swimming pools on board. Some are so big they even have miniature golf courses and waterparks! The largest cruise ship in the world is called *Harmony of the Seas* — it can carry more than 6500 passengers!

Didgeridoo
A wind instrument traditionally used by the aboriginal people of Australia, made from a hollow branch. It has a very deep low sound. When it's played in a subway station, it almost feels like the walls are vibrating.

Express train
A passenger train that makes fewer stops than a regular train and gets you to your destination faster. That means you might be skipping some transfer stops — which is good for most people if they're traveling a long distance, but not for Secret Agent Rybka!

Fare
The money you have to pay to ride public transit. In some cities, the fare depends on how far you travel. In others, a single fare pays for travel over any distance within a set period of time.

Ferry

A boat or ship that carries passengers and goods over a short distance. Some ferries can also carry cars, and others even have rail tracks to take trains on board. Transit riding on transit!

Guide dog (or service dog)

A dog whose job it is to help someone who is blind or has another disability. Guide dogs can also help people with certain mental illnesses. They go through a lot of training for their big job. They learn to guide their owners around obstacles, keep them safe in traffic, help them get dressed and much more.

License

A legal document that gives a person permission to do something, such as drive a car or boat or become a public transit driver.

Light rail transit (or LRT)

Electricity-powered urban tram that has its own lane. It's also often called fast tram, rapid transit, light metro or light rail train.

Lost and Found

When something is left behind on a bus or train, it often ends up in the Lost and Found. People can call or visit the Lost and Found to check if their lost item is there. Lost and found things include umbrellas, phones, hats, gloves, books and even didgeridoos.

Observatory

A building with a large telescope and a roof that opens up and lets you see, or observe, the stars. The world's largest telescope is being built in Chile. It will spend 10 years observing billions of stars and galaxies and taking pictures of the universe.

Population

The number of people living in a place. The world's most populated cities are: Tokyo (Japan), Delhi (India), Shanghai (China) and Mexico City (Mexico).

Priority seat

Priority seats are reserved for passengers with special needs, to give them easy access to the door. Passengers with special needs include people with disabilities, elderly people, expecting mothers and parents with young children.

Public transit (or public transportation)

Buses, trains, subways and other forms of transportation that move people (the public) on specific routes within and around the city for a set fare. Public transit helps reduce traffic and pollution and leave more room for parks, bike paths and playgrounds. It's also usually less expensive than driving a car or taking a taxi.

Resident

A person who lives somewhere permanently as opposed to just visiting. Residents of New York City are called New Yorkers. Residents of Liverpool are called Liverpudlians! What are residents called where you live?

Signal

A light that's used to let drivers know if they should stop or go. There are signals that direct regular traffic on roads and signals that direct trains, such as the ones in the subway tunnels.

Smart card

A plastic card that you can buy and use for your fare instead of cash money. For example, you can buy a $20 card and use it for $20 worth of transit rides, just by scanning it at the fare box every time you get on. Once the $20 runs out, you can add more money to the card and use it again. Smart, right?

Spy

A person who secretly collects and reports information. Some of the information spies collect is very important and must be kept secret. That's why spies sometimes need to pretend they are someone else.

Subway

An underground train system that moves passengers in large cities. The world's deepest subway is in Pyongyang, North Korea. It's about 110 m (360 ft.) deep!

Subway line

A route in the subway system, usually marked by its own color on the subway map.

Transfer station

A subway station that's shared by two or more subway lines, and where passengers can change from one line to another.

Transit hub

A station where different types of public transit meet and passengers can switch from one type to another. For example, you could arrive by train, then get on a subway or a light rail train. That is, of course, if you paid the right fare!

Water taxi

A small motorboat used to transport passengers over short stretches of water, such as rivers or canals, or between city islands.